# Timeline of engineering

Since ancient times, engineers have expe
with new inventions and technologies. Take a look
at how engineering has changed since 530 BCE!

## Smart machine
American George Deval
builds Unimate, the first
industrial robotic arm.

Apollo 11 spacecraft
on the Moon.

## First flight
The Wright
brothers make
the first manned
flight in a
powered and
controllable
aircraft.

Unimate 2000B robot

## Moon
landing
Humankind
lands on
the Moon.

## Solar panels
Tiles that can collect
the Sun's energy are
mass-produced for
the first time.

| 1903 | 1908 | 1914 | 1956 | 1969 | 1998 | 2012 | 2016 |

## Cars for
everyone
American
businessman
Henry Ford
builds the
Model T car
using mass-
produced parts.

## Panama Canal
Engineer John Frank
Stevens designs the
Panama Canal, a
huge waterway
that connects the
Atlantic and
Pacific oceans.

## ISS
The International
Space Station (ISS)
is launched into
low Earth orbit.

## Mars rover
A sky crane
lowers the
Curiosity rover
onto the surface
of Mars.

Sky crane in action

Model T Ford, 1911

Things to find out:

# DK findout!

# Engineering

Author: Emily Hunt

**DK** | Penguin Random House

**Senior editors** Lizzie Davey, Garima Sharma
**Senior art editor** Katie Knutton
**Project editor** Satu Fox
**Project art editor** Nidhi Mehra
**Editor** Radhika Haswani
**Art editor** Radhika Banerjee
**Editorial assistants** Sarah Foakes, Megan Weal
**Design assistant** Ala Uddin
**Managing editor** Laura Gilbert
**Deputy managing editor** Vineetha Mokkil
**Managing art editors** Diane Peyton Jones,
Neha Ahuja Chowdhry
**Picture researcher** Sakshi Saluja
**Pre-production producer** Nadine King
**Producer** Isabell Schart
**Art director** Martin Wilson
**Publisher** Sarah Larter
**Publishing director** Sophie Mitchell
**Educational consultant** Jacqueline Harris

First published in Great Britain in 2017 by
Dorling Kindersley Limited
80 Strand, London, WC2R 0RL

Copyright © 2017 Dorling Kindersley Limited
A Penguin Random House Company
10 9 8 7 6 5 4 3 2 1
001–299032–July/2017

A CIP catalogue record for this book
is available from the British Library.
ISBN: 978-0-2412-8509-1

Printed and bound in China

A WORLD OF IDEAS:
**SEE ALL THERE IS TO KNOW**
www.dk.com

# Contents

**4** What is an engineer?

**6** First engineers

**8** Genius inventor

**10** Problem solving

**12** Materials

**14** Machines

**16** Cars

**18** Power

**20** Robots

**22** Incredible engineers

**24** Extreme machines

Roman crane

3D printer

6 Roller coasters

8 Flying machines

10 The Wright brothers

12 Jet engines

14 Nanotechnology

16 Space engineers

18 Mix it up!

20 Building our world

22 Underground

24 Eiffel Tower

26 Skyscrapers

48 Building bridges

50 Meet the expert

52 Bioengineering

54 Going green

56 Future engineering

58 Engineering facts and figures

60 Glossary

62 Index

64 Acknowledgements

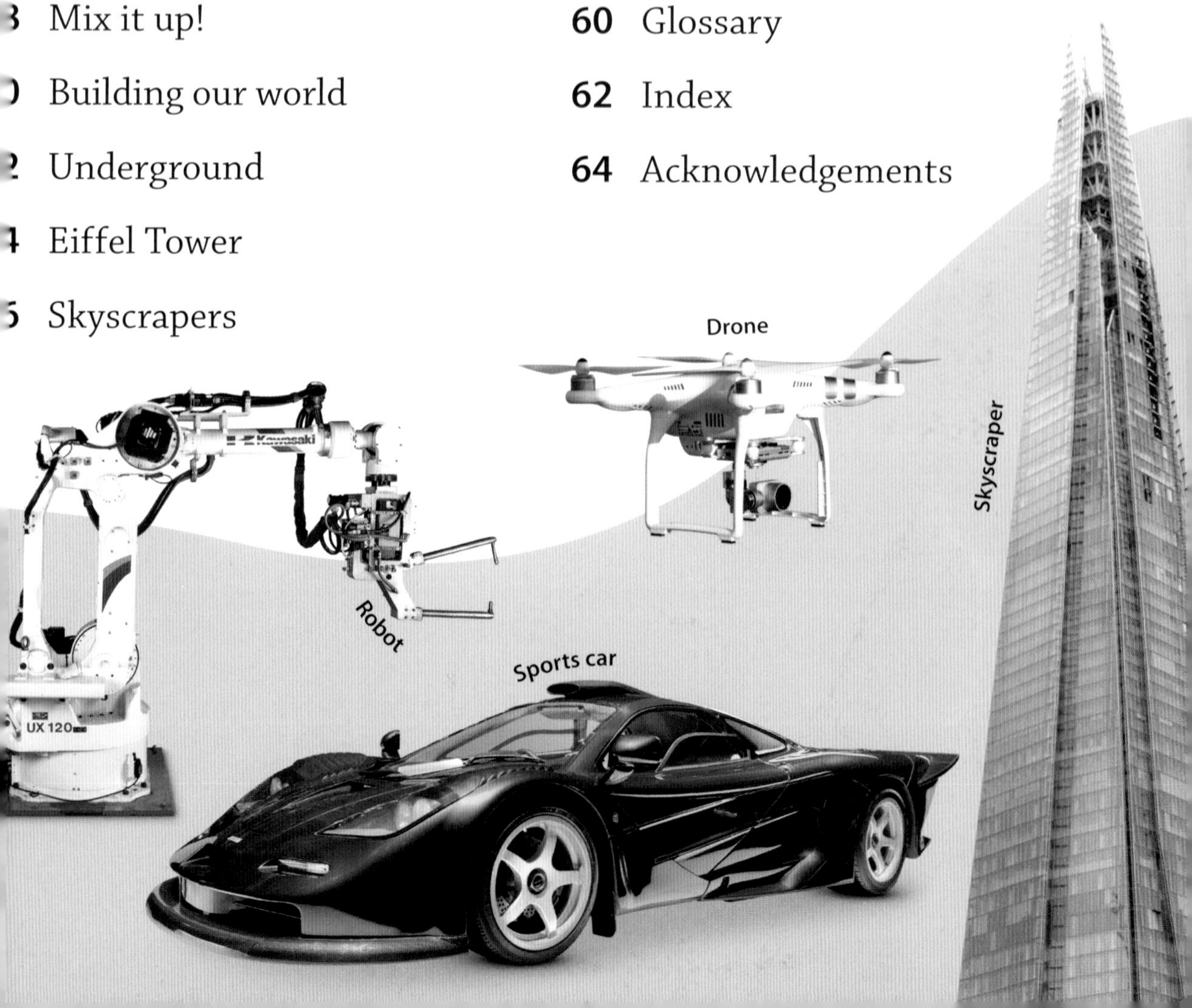

Drone

Skyscraper

Robot

Sports car

# What is an engineer?

An engineer is a problem solver. Engineers use maths and science to build things – from the tiniest particles to the tallest buildings. They invent new technologies, and make existing technologies even better.

## New ideas

Engineers come up with ideas for new inventions, and make existing designs better. Your idea could lead to a medical device that helps cure an illness, a spacecraft that carries humans to Mars, a new clean power source, or an earthquake.

Testing the design of an Olympic bicycle in a wind tunnel

Engineer working on an airplane engine

## Creative approaches

Being an engineer means coming up with solutions to difficult problems. Having studied maths and science, engineers use their knowledge to design new systems and products that could change lives, from earthquake-proof buildings to cures for deadly diseases.

# Engineers everywhere

Engineering is an exciting job if you love adventure. An engineer might create a new design on a computer and then get to travel to all sorts of places to help it be built and tested. Engineers work on giant jet engines, at the very top of wind turbines, under the ocean, and even in space!

An engineer at work on the International Space Station

Testing an undersea power cable on the beach in Zanzibar

## Around the world

Engineers work in every country on the planet. While the building materials, landscapes, and problems that they face may be different, engineers use the same creativity and problem-solving methods wherever they work.

# How do I become an engineer?

While you are at school, you'll learn a lot of the maths and science you need. Later, you can go to university and study engineering. Most importantly, keep dreaming of new ways of solving problems!

# First engineers

Ancient engineers had only simple tools to work with, but they built some of the world's most famous buildings, from the Pyramids in Egypt to the Parthenon in Greece. Some simple machines invented in ancient times include the lever, the crane, and the first clocks.

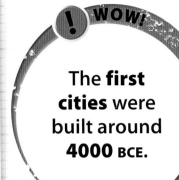

**! WOW!**

The **first cities** were built around **4000** BCE.

## Ancient clock

Water clocks are one of the oldest ways of telling time. The hours could be measured because the water always took the same length of time to drip from one tank to another.

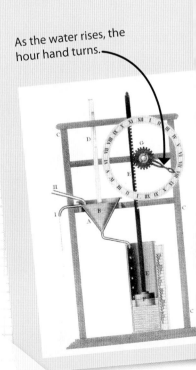

As the water rises, the hour hand turns.

## Roman crane

Cranes use pulleys to lift heavy loads. It is easier to pull down on a rope to move something than to lift it by hand. The Romans used cranes to lift stone when they were building structures such as the Colosseum in Rome.

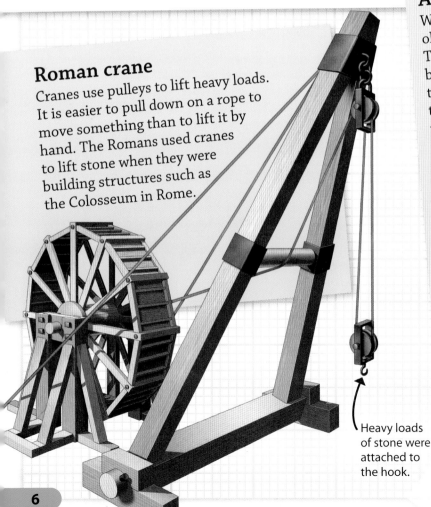

Heavy loads of stone were attached to the hook.

# Useful levers

Levers are bars that rest on a point called a fulcrum. They make it easier to push or lift weights. The long handles of a wheelbarrow act as a lever, with the wheel as the fulcrum. Wheelbarrows were invented in China around 220 BCE.

The wheel acts as a fulcrum.

The handles act as a lever to lift the load.

# Wheeled chariot

The wheel was invented around 3500 BCE. At first, wheels were heavy and only used on slow-moving carts. By 1600 BCE, the Ancient Egyptians had invented fast chariots that could be pulled into battle by horses. One soldier drove the chariot and another one fired arrows.

Using spokes instead of solid wood made wheels lighter.

# Water lifter

The Archimedean screw is an Ancient Egyptian invention for lifting water. A wooden spiral is built inside a tube, with one end in the water. When the handle is turned, the water is trapped in the spiral and lifted to the top.

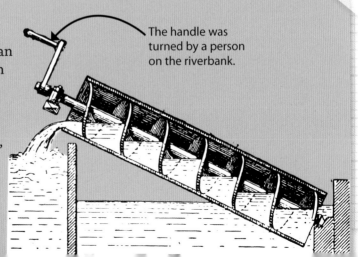

The handle was turned by a person on the riverbank.

7

# Genius inventor

Leonardo da Vinci is best known as the artist who painted the *Mona Lisa* but he was also a self-taught engineer. He was fascinated by how everything worked – from the human body to military machines. Here, we imagine what an interview with da Vinci might have been like.

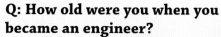

**FACT FILE**

» **Name:** Leonardo da V

» **Dates:** 1452–1519

» **Location:** Vinci, Italy

» **Fun fact:** Da Vinci love all animals. He bought caged birds so that he could set them free.

**Q: How old were you when you became an engineer?**

**A:** I didn't get an engineering job until I was 30 years old. After that, I worked a a military engineer for 17 years in the city of Milan, Italy.

**Q: How did you get your first job as an engineer?**

**A:** In the 1480s, the people of Milan needed help because they were at wa with the city of Venice. I wrote to Duke Sforza telling him about my military inventions, such as a huge cannon. He loved my ideas!

**Q: Why were you interested in engineering when you were already an artist?**

**A:** It's as much fun to design amazing machines as it is to paint people and landscapes. I can use my drawing and designing skills to design my engineering projects. Also, engineers are paid a lot mor than artists in the 15th century!

## Q: What are your favourite projects?

**A:** I designed weapons such as tanks, catapults, submarines, and machine guns. I also worked on better levers, gears, and cranes. But my favourite inventions include machines for flying and breathing underwater.

## Q: Some people say you have designed a self-moving machine. Is this true?

**A:** Yes! In 1495, I came up with plans for a wind-up, self-moving machine with three wheels. I didn't manage to make it work in real life, though.

## Q: What is your greatest weakness as an engineer?

**A:** I am easily distracted by new ideas, and I often leave projects unfinished. I only managed to finish 17 paintings.

Da Vinci's design for a parachute, made from wood and cloth.

In 2000, da Vinci's parachute was finally built and floated safely down 3 km (2 miles).

## Q: What do you think is the most important skill for a good engineer?

**A:** Creativity and imagination! Engineers must be able to look at a project that has already been started and see how to make it even better in the future.

## Q: Did any of your projects fail?

**A:** My design for a huge statue of a horse was ready to be built when Duke Sforza gave all the bronze away! He used it to bribe an enemy army not to attack Milan.

Da Vinci designed this catapult like a giant crossbow.

Da Vinci wrote backwards to keep his thoughts secret.

**1**

How did the Romans get water to their towns and cities?

**2**

How can food be kept cool?

**3**

How can we turn wind energy into electricity?

**4**

How can more buildings be built if there isn't any room left in a city?

**A**

## Wind turbines

A wind turbine captures energy and turns it into electricity. The electricity is made when wind turns the blades of the turbine.

**B**

## Satellites

A satellite sends live TV signals and telephone calls around the world. Satellites in space are linked to some on Earth, which pick up signals and turn them into pictures and sounds.

## Hudson Yards

This group of new buildings is being built on top of a railway line i New York. It will includ hotels, shops, schools, houses, and parks.

**F**

# Problem solving

Engineers look at the problems that we face in everyday life and try to make our lives more comfortable, quicker, and easier. Engineers have solved problems like keeping cool in the summer, developing energy from nature, getting food from farms to shops, flying, and exploring space. Take the quiz to match the problem with its invention.

**5**
How can we get people to and from the International Space Station?

**6**
How do the pictures get onto our television screens?

**! WOW!**
Engineers can remove **salt** from **seawater** so it can be used for **drinking.**

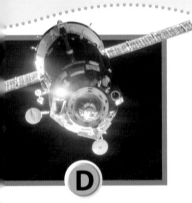

**D**

### *Soyuz* craft
The *Soyuz* craft can carry three people into space. It also carries food and water.

**C**

### Refrigerator
A refrigerator works by changing a substance called a coolant from a liquid to a gas and back again. This series of changes keeps the space cold and food fresh.

**E**

### Aqueducts
An aqueduct is designed to carry water slowly from a hillside into a town.

### Changing ideas
The "Walkie Talkie'" skyscraper in London was designed with a curved shape that reflected the Sun's rays and accidentally melted part of a car. Engineers designed a protective shade for the building to solve the problem.

Sun's rays

Curved face

Heat builds up in a small area.

The "Walkie Talkie", London

# Materials

Everything around us is made from something. We call these somethings "materials". Engineers create, change, and test materials that we use every day. Our phones, cars, and even babies' nappies are all made from carefully chosen, specially engineered materials.

## Plastic

Plastics are manufactured materials. They are cheap t produce and have insulatin properties, which means they keep heat in or out.

## Ceramics

Ceramics are materials formed at very high temperatures. Most ceramics are very hard, but brittle, which means they break easily.

Some engine parts are made from ceramics.

## Fabric

Engineers can create fabrics with special abilities. For example, fabrics that block harmful rays from the Sun. Some clothing is designed to pull sweat away from the body, using tiny threads that are very close together.

## Metal
Metals have a solid structure, which makes them strong. They can be bent into many different shapes – from staircases to long thin wires. Metals conduct electricity, which means an electric current can move through them.

## Composite
A composite material is created when two or more materials are combined to make a new one. Engineers make composite materials that are strong but very light.

## Wood
Wood is a natural material from trees. Engineers add other materials to the surface of wood to stop it from rotting. Wood is used as a building material all over the world.

## Concrete
Concrete is used for many structures, such as buildings, bridges, and streets, because it can hold heavy weights without being crushed. It is made from a mixture of cement, stones, and water.

# Machines

Machines can do tasks that are too tiny, huge, boring, or dangerous for humans. Some machines can be controlled by a human, such as a kitchen blender. Others can be programmed to follow instructions without human control, such as driverless vehicles.

Digger with crane arm

Formula 1 car

### Engine

A car's engine burns fuel to spin its wheels, moving it forward much faster than a human could possibly run. Formula 1 racing cars use very powerful fuel, and can travel at up to 231 mph (372 kph).

## ...ane arm

...using levers and hydraulic power
...ater pressure), crane arms are able to
... much more weight than humans
...ld ever manage.

## Robotic arm

Robot arms can precisely grip and
lift small parts, so they are useful for
making goods such as cars. Robots can
make the same movements hundreds
of times, without getting tired or
making mistakes.

Sending out packages

## Driverless tractor

Driverless technology
allows farmers to mow
and plant their fields
from home! They put
instructions into a
computer, and then the
tractor does all the work.

Self-driving tractor

# Cars

The first car was made over 120 years ago. It was called the Benz Motorwagen, had three wheels, and could only go as fast as 10 kph (6 mph). Modern cars have four wheels and can reach speeds of up to 439 kph (273 mph). Engineers are always developing cars that are safer, more environmentally friendly, and that cost less to run.

## Fit for purpose

Cars are used for lots of diffe... tasks. Some need to be able ... go very fast, carry a lot of pe... or move heavy materials a lo... way. Engineers keep these specific needs in mind when they design a car.

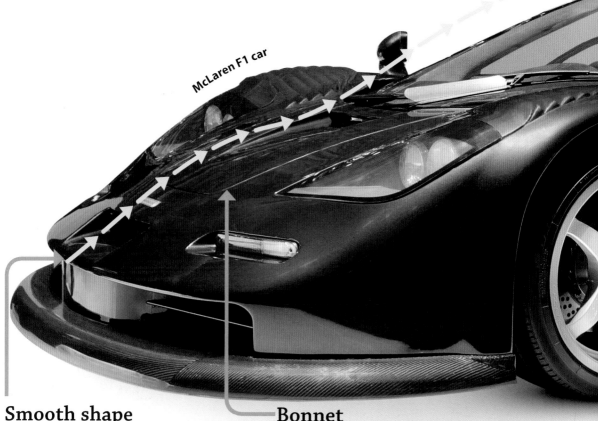

McLaren F1 car

## Smooth shape

The car has a smooth shape so that air can pass easily over the body. This lets the car travel faster.

## Bonnet

In most cars the engine is under a lid, called the bonnet. In the McLaren F1, the bonnet has a gold layer inside, which protects the car from the heat of the engine.

### Battery powered

Engineers have created cars that run off big rechargeable batteries. These batteries are charged by electricity. They are better for the environment because they do not release any gas.

Electric car

Off road driving on sand dunes.

### Tricky terrain

For tough, bumpy surfaces cars need to have a special design and shape. They have big tyres that are higher off the ground. This keeps them more stable and makes sure they don't trip over any obstacles.

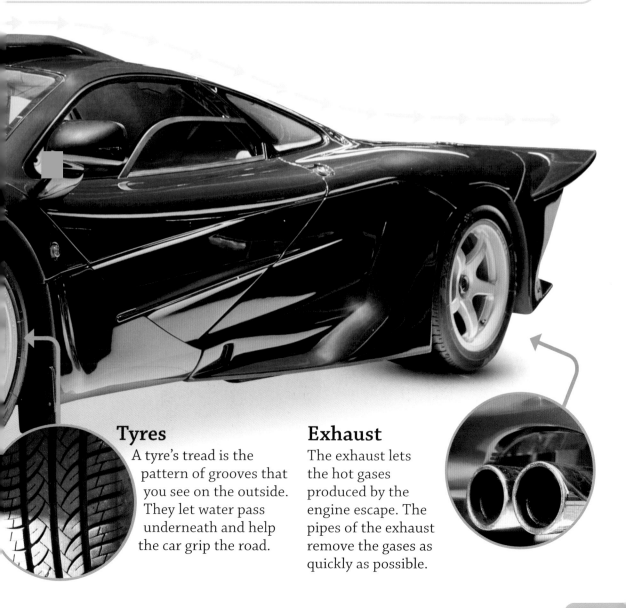

## Tyres

A tyre's tread is the pattern of grooves that you see on the outside. They let water pass underneath and help the car grip the road.

## Exhaust

The exhaust lets the hot gases produced by the engine escape. The pipes of the exhaust remove the gases as quickly as possible.

# Power

We need electricity to run most machines – from ovens to space rockets. Engineers design and build the different structures that create electricity. Most electricity is made in large power stations from burning fossil fuels, or using renewable sources such as wind or water power. Steam is created that then turns a turbine, a machine with blades that spins so quickly it can create electricity.

## Power networks

Electricity is transported from power stations to homes and offices through aluminium cables. They are held above the ground by metal towers called electricity pylons.

**Electricity pylons**

## Fossil fuels

Coal, gas, and oil are all fossil fuels. These made up of the squashed remains of plants and animals. When they are burned, they heat up water to create steam, which then turns a turbine.

## Water power

Water flowing downhill can turn a turbine create power. Engineers make use of this b building dams with turbines in them. Ocea waves and currents can also be used.

## Wind power

The arms of wind turbines turn when the v blows, which creates electricity. Large turb create a lot more power. Modern turbines be more than 100 m (328 ft) tall!

## Solar power

Solar panels are made up of cells that abso sunlight. The light is then turned into electricity. Solar panels work best where there is lots of sunlight and hardly any clo

## Geothermal power

Geothermal power uses the natural heat of the Earth. One way to create power is to pump cold water deep under the Earth's surface, where it is so hot it turns into the steam needed to turn a turbine.

## Nuclear power

Nuclear power uses a process called fission where atoms are split apart. The heat this creates boils water to make steam, which then turns turbines to produce electricity.

**Coal power station**
The white smoke rising from the towers of coal power stations is steam from the boiling water used to turn the turbines that make electricity.

**Hydroelectric dam**
Dams turn rivers into lakes, which create higher pressure. The weight of the water rotates turbines inside the dam.

**Wind farm**
Groups of wind turbines are called wind farms. They are built where there are few people and strong winds. Some are even built out at sea.

**Solar farm**
The energy produced from a single solar panel is very small. Solar farms have large groups of solar panels, called arrays.

**Geothermal power**
Places like Iceland and Japan have hot areas under the Earth's surface. This makes it easier to heat up water to create geothermal power.

**Nuclear reactor**
Six grams (1/3 oz) of nuclear fuel can make as much energy as 1 tonne (1.1 ston) of coal. However, the uranium used to make nuclear fuel is rare.

## Humanoids

Humanoid robots look and move like humans. They can work with tools and let engineers learn more about how the human body works and moves. A humanoid with a human face is called an android.

## Robot workers

Robots can be used to do jobs that need carefulness and speed. They are used to buil cars, carry out surgery, and harvest food on farms. Some of these robots are controlled b humans, while others can work on their own

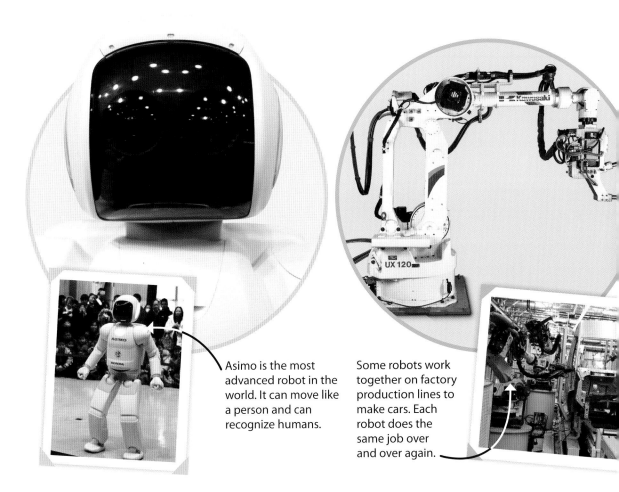

Asimo is the most advanced robot in the world. It can move like a person and can recognize humans.

Some robots work together on factory production lines to make cars. Each robot does the same job over and over again.

# Robots

Robots are machines that are built by engineers to do jobs and perform actions that would otherwise be done by a human. Robots do the things that people do, but with more force and speed, and more precisely. There are more than a million robots in the world – they are all around us!

## ˻bot body parts

˻gineers have created robotic body parts
˻t can be attached to humans. These
˻ootic body parts are called prosthetics.
˻ey are controlled by the brain of the
˻son wearing them.

## Hard to reach

Robots can reach places that humans
can't. They are used underwater, in space,
and underground, as these places can be
dangerous for humans. They find objects,
collect data, and take pictures.

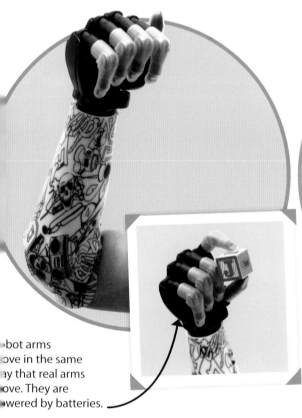

˻bot arms
˻ove in the same
˻y that real arms
˻ove. They are
˻wered by batteries.

Kurt I is a robot that
works in the sewers.
It makes sure
everything is working
properly and fixes
things that aren't.

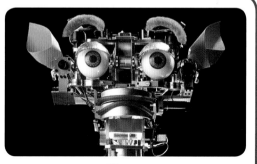

## ˻Robots with feelings

˻he big difference between robots and
˻umans is that humans have emotions.
˻ngineers have made robots that respond
˻o a human's feelings. One of these robots,
˻ismet, responds to the feelings of the
˻erson it is communicating with by moving
˻ts face and changing the tone of its voice.

**Kismet**

# Incredible engineers

Everything around us started out as an idea. Great thinkers have dreamt up new inventions to improve our daily lives – and they continue to do so. From early machines and basic technologies to soaring skyscrapers and futuristic robots, the engineering industry continues to shape our world.

## George Stephenson

Known as the "Father of Railways", George Stephenson (1781–1848) designed and built the first commercial locomotive. The *Rocket* was the first vehicle to go faster than a horse, at 47 kph (29 mph).

A working replica of Stephenson's *Rocket*

## Lillian Moller Gilbreth

Engineer Gilbreth (1878–1972) improved the layout of kitchens in America and the efficiency of household items. She was the first woman elected into the National Academy of Engineering.

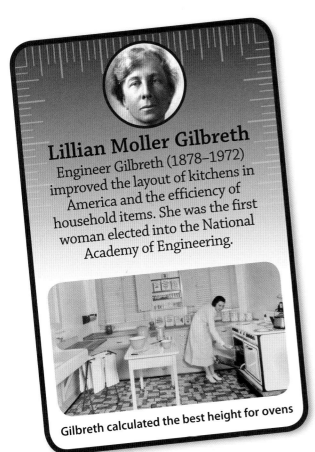

Gilbreth calculated the best height for ovens

## Yoky Matsuoka

Computer scientist Yoky Matsuoka (1972–) is using robotic technology to help disabled people become more mobile. Her model of a robot hand is the first step in creating a prosthetic hand controlled by the brain.

Matsuoka's ground-breaking robotic hand

## Isambard Kingdom Brunel

Engineer Brunel (1806–1859) designed and built ships, bridges, and railways. His *SS Great Britain* was the first iron steamship with a propeller to cross the Atlantic. He also worked on the first tunnel to be built underwater.

*SS Great Britain*

## Alexander Graham Bell

After working as a speech therapist for deaf people, scientist Alexander Graham Bell (1847–1922) invented the telephone. Speech could be sent along wires for the first time, changing the way we communicate.

A man uses one of Bell's first telephones

## Dr Maggie Aderin-Pocock

Space engineer Dr Maggie Aderin-Pocock (1968–) works on satellites that gather information on climate change. She also invented a tool for the huge Gemini Telescope, which is 8.1 m (26.6 ft) wide.

The Gemini Telescope in Chile

**! WOW!**

Bell's first telephone message was to his assistant: "Mr Watson, come here! I want to see you!"

# Extreme machines

These amazing machines are all extremely big, heavy, or powerful. This means they are perfectly suited to doing certain jobs, such as lifting, carrying, or drilling.

## GIANT DRILL

Tunnel boring machines are used to dig giant tunnels underground for roads and railways. The largest one in the world is named Bertha. It can drill or bore a hole as tall as a five-storey building.

## Road train

Some Australian outback trucks can pull three long trailers. These megatrucks, called road trains, can be as long as two basketball courts and carry the equivalent weight of 40 elephants!

## NUCLEAR SUBMARINE

The Russian Typhoon Class are the world's biggest submarines. They are 175 m (574 ft) in length – longer than five blue whales. They can stay underwater for four months at a time, are nuclear-powered, and carry weapons like missiles.

# Super Guppy

This enormous but strange-looking plane was built by NASA to transport large cargo, such as satellites, rockets, and smaller planes. It opens in the middle, allowing the cargo on and off.

# GANTRY CRANE

The largest crane in the world is the Taisun gantry crane, currently in Sandong Province, China. It can lift 19,600 tonnes (22,000 tons), and is used to move large materials around and build boats in shipyards.

# HADRON COLLIDER

This particle accelerator is used for physics experiments that try to understand how the world began and what it is made out of. It uses magnets to "shoot" particles extremely fast, and is the world's biggest machine. It is in Switzerland and is almost entirely underground.

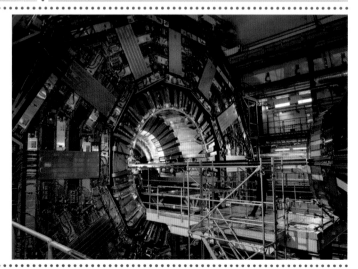

# Supercarrier

The American Nimitz Class are the world's largest aircraft carriers. Carrying over 6,000 people, they can go 20 years without refuelling. The flight deck holds more than 60 aircraft!

**Going uphill**
There is only one motor in a roller coaster. It moves the carriage up the first slope.

**Roller coaster carriage**
The carriage of the roller coaster holds the riders. There is no engine on a roller coaster carriage – it runs on the energy it transfers as the carriage goes up and down hills and loops.

**Nuts and bolts**
Large rollercoasters are held together with more than 60,000 bolts.

# Roller coasters

Engineers create complicated and careful designs to make roller coasters safe and fun. Mechanical, electrical, and structural engineers all work together to imagine, design, and build these exciting machines.

**Upside down**

The **Kingda Ka** in the **USA** is the tallest roller coaster in the world. Its tallest point is **139 m (456 ft)** from the ground!

**Wheels**
Wheels prevent the carriage from wobbling and falling off the track.

**Brakes**
Roller coasters have magnetic, automatic breaks so that the carriages can be stopped.

**Thrill ride**
When you are upside down on a roller coaster, you are being pushed and pulled around by different forces. Gravity is trying to pull you out of your seat, but acceleration pushes you into your seat. This is why you end up feeling weightless.

Early roller coaster

**Wooden coasters**
The first roller coasters were called switchback railways. They were made of wood, didn't have loops, and were much slower and shorter than modern roller coasters.

# Flying machines

Flying machines are usually known as aircraft. They include planes, helicopters, gliders, and drones. Aircraft have come a long way since the Wright brothers made their first flight in 1903. They can now fly all the way around the world.

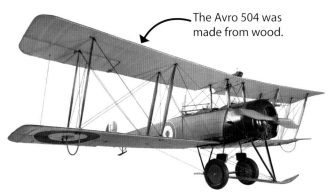

The Avro 504 was made from wood.

## Avro 504

The Avro 504 was used for bombing and spying by the British in World War I. It was a biplane, which means an aircraft with two wings stacked one above the other.

## Flight design CTSW

This aircraft is built from light, strong materials called composites. It has a very large fuel tank.

Light materials help aircraft fly long distances.

## Hawker Harrier

The Hawker jet aircraft can take off straight up into the air! It is also called the Jump Jet.

Downward-facing engines help the plane take off.

# obinson R44

elicopters can fly up and
own, as well as forwards.
ey can be used for rescuing people or
rrying heavy loads. R44 helicopters
ve a fuel container designed to
rvive a crash.

### ACT FILE

▶ **Year:** 1993
▶ **Speed:** 240 kph (149 mph)
▶ **Fun fact:** The Robinson R44
s the world's bestselling
rivate helicopter.

# -22 Osprey

is aircraft is a tiltrotor
craft. That means it has
tors that can face upwards
fly like a helicopter, or
wards to fly like a plane.

### ACT FILE

▶ **Year:** 2007
▶ **Speed:** 565 kph (351 mph)
▶ **Fun fact:** The V-22 Osprey
an be folded so it can be
tored on ships.

The Osprey can carry
32 passengers.

# JI Phantom 3

drone is an aircraft that
flown remotely by a pilot.
gineers have created drones
travel into dangerous areas,
ch as erupting volcanoes.

### FACT FILE

》 **Year:** 2015
》 **Speed:** 57 kph (35 mph)
》 **Fun fact:** Farmers can use
drones to find out if their
crops have enough water.

Drones can have
cameras mounted
underneath.

# The Wright brothers

Orville and Wilbur Wright invented the world's first aeroplane. In 1903, the Wright Flyer made its first flight and changed the way that people travelled. The brothers tested and invented every part of their flying machines so well that many of their ideas are still used today.

Orville and Wilbur became interested in engineering when they were children and their father bought them a flying toy.

In 1892, the Wrights started their first engineering business, making and selling bicycles. They soon decided to aim for the sky.

The pair wanted to build a flying machine. They studied birds and learned about how their wings worked. They noticed that the wings moved in different parts.

To test their ideas, the brothers built a wind tunnel. These tests meant that they could study how wings would work in the air.

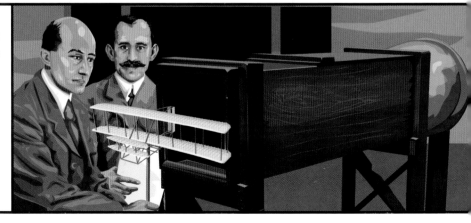

Next, the Wright others designed glider that had narrow wings with parts that could be controlled by the pilot. This meant that the pilot could steer the aeroplane up and down, and left to right.

Once the wings were finished, the brothers added an engine to create the Wright Flyer. They tested it at Kitty Hawk in North Carolina. It only flew 37 m (120 ft), but they'd done it!

In 1909, the brothers set up the Wright Company. They made planes and trained pilots.

The Wright Flyer changed the way that people travelled forever. Many of the brothers' discoveries are still used when building aeroplanes and space shuttles today.

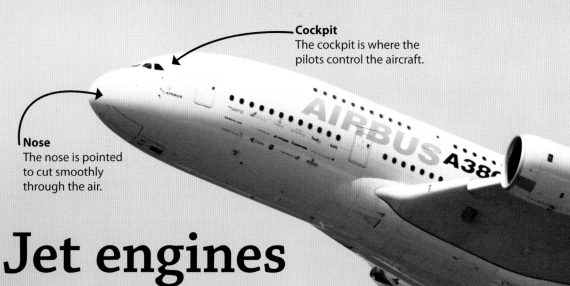

**Cockpit**
The cockpit is where the pilots control the aircraft.

**Nose**
The nose is pointed to cut smoothly through the air.

**Engines**
Several engines are needed to power the heavy plane.

# Jet engines

Planes fly using thrust and lift. Thrust is created in the engines by pushing air and hot gases out of the back at high speeds. This pushes the plane forwards. Lift keeps the aircraft in the air and is created by air rushing over the wing that pulls the plane up.

## Jumbo jet engines

Jumbo jets get their name from their huge size, which means they need large engines, too. A passenger liner carries up to 200,000 litres (54,000 gallons) of fuel on long flights.

This fan is 3 m (10²/₅ ft) wide

## Fan blades

Jumbo jet engines have huge fans that suck in cold air. The fan blades are made from a strong metal called titanium.

**Wings**
The wings provide lift, which keeps the jet in the air.

A380

F-WWOW

**Contrails**
Burning fuel and air creates white streaks of vapour called contrails.

# How does a jet engine work?

The jet engine is a type of engine that uses air mixed with fuel. It is also known as a turbofan. The engine takes in air, mixes it with fuel, and burns the mixture to create thrust.

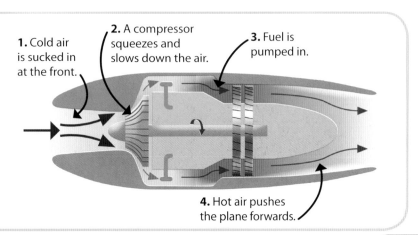

**1.** Cold air is sucked in at the front.

**2.** A compressor squeezes and slows down the air.

**3.** Fuel is pumped in.

**4.** Hot air pushes the plane forwards.

# Nanotechnology

Nanotechnology is engineering on a scale so tiny it can't even be seen with a normal microscope. Engineers work at this scale to tackle very small problems like bacteria in the body or rain getting your clothes wet. Eventually, they hope to create machines so small they can travel inside your body to release medicine exactly where it is needed.

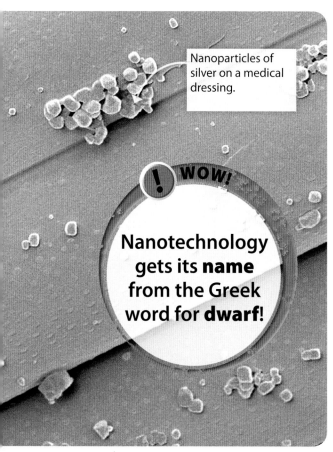

Nanoparticles of silver on a medical dressing.

**WOW!**

Nanotechnology gets its **name** from the Greek word for **dwarf!**

**Sun protection**
Sunblock cream can be made from nanoparticles of special chemicals that absorb harmful UV light from the Sun. Their tiny size means they are transparent and m... the cream feel very light on your skin.

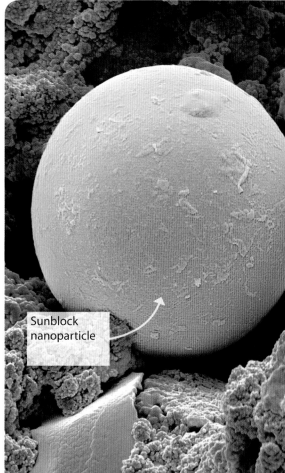

Sunblock nanoparticle

**Antibacterial bandages**
Silver nanoparticles kill bacteria. Doctors and nurses use liquid silver as a treatment to stop wounds from getting infected. Engineers can now make bandages with silver nanoparticles in them, which are easier to use.

# How small is a nanoparticle?

A nanometre is one-millionth of a millimetre. Objects on the nanoscale are less than 100 nm (nanometres) in length. They can only be seen through very powerful microscopes.

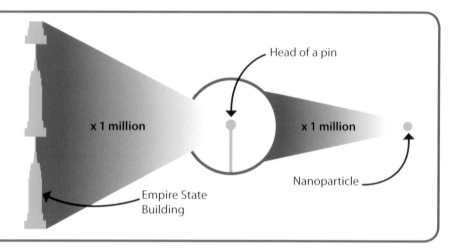

Head of a pin

x 1 million

x 1 million

Nanoparticle

Empire State Building

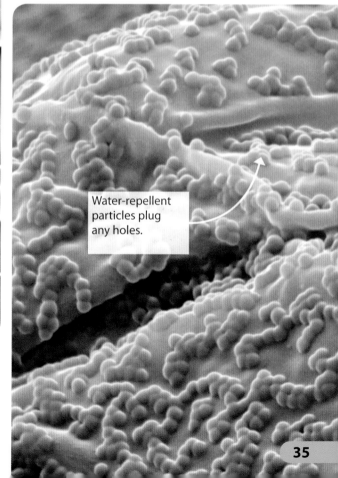

Structure of graphene atoms

Water-repellent particles plug any holes.

## Water-repellent fabric

Nanoparticles of silicone can be added to fabrics to make them completely waterproof. Because nanoparticles are so tiny, they can completely cover any holes in the fabric's surface and block water from being absorbed.

## Super-strong material

The strongest, thinnest, lightest material that engineers have created so far is called graphene. It is 200 times stronger than steel and is made from a single layer of pure carbon atoms (tiny particles that make up all materials) arranged in a honeycomb pattern.

# Space engineers

Travelling into space is one of the greatest engineering achievements in history. Every tiny thing that travels into space is carefully designed by huge teams of scientists and engineers, to make space travel as safe and problem-free as possible.

**Special materials**
The materials that are used in space need to be strong, and able to survive extreme temperatures. They also need to be light enough to be taken into space.

**Robot arm**
Large robotic arms are used to move huge objects and astronauts into very precise locations.

**Solar arrays**
The solar arrays on the International Space Station (I gather energy from the Sun a convert it into electricity. The cover an area bigger than the length of two tennis courts.

# Exploring space

Clever engineering lets us visit and explore space. We even send machines to planets that humans cannot land on yet.

**Back and forth**
Space shuttles were used to carry astronauts and equipment into space. US space shuttles have carried out 135 missions into space, with each shuttle take-off generating as much power as 15,000 train engines.

US space shuttle

*Curiosity's* mast holds seven cameras.

*Curiosity* rover

**Spacesuit**
An astronaut's spacesuit protects them in space. Space objects fly very fast, so even small bits of dust could injure an unprotected astronaut. Spacesuits also provide astronauts with oxygen, water, and protection from the Sun.

**Life on Mars**
A rover is a large robot that drives around a planet taking pictures and collecting data for scientists to study. There are currently four active rovers on the surface of Mars.

# Mix it up!

Chemical engineers use chemicals to make new products, and to make existing products better. Natural chemicals come from plants and animals, while synthetic chemicals are created in laboratories. When chemicals are mixed together, they react and change. Everyday things, such as medicines, toilet paper, and plastic, are all created by chemical engineering.

## Medicine

Chemical engineers use natural and synthe chemicals to make medic They experiment to find which chemicals make p better, and what treatm work best, so that peo can live longer and healthier lives.

## Environment

Chemical engineers help to keep the environment clean. They work to improve recycling, clean up oil spills, and build systems to reduce harmful gas formation.

## Food and drink

Some food products are engineered. Preservatives, flavouring, dyes, and vitamins are added to food. They can make it last longer, and taste and look nicer.

## Materials

Engineers develop materials that work in different ways. Plastic can be changed into many forms. For example, it can be used for packaging, fabrics, and building.

## Energy

Engineers have developed ways to get energy from different sources, such as coal, gas, the Sun, and wind. They are now trying to work out how to get energy from plants.

## Clothes

Clothes are designed for exact uses, such as to be waterproof or warm. The special materials used in waterproof clothing are designed so that water slides off them. They are created using synthetic chemicals.

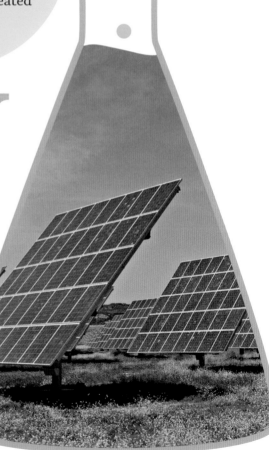

# Building our world

Have you ever walked over a bridge, drunk water from a tap, or taken a train? These are all things that civil engineers make happen. They help design and construct things that make the everyday life of the whole world go smoothly.

## Tunnels

Instead of building a road over an obstacle, it may be safer or cheaper to build a tunnel through or under it. Civil engineers also keep people safe while they are in the tunnel, by building in lights and a good flow of air.

» **Name:** Gotthard Base Tunnel, Switzerla

» **Name:** Pan-American Highway, USA

## Roads

Roads play an important role in every country. In t USA, there are over 6.5 million km (4 million mil of road. Engineers decide what materials to build roads from so that they w last a long time.

## Canals

Networks of canals allow boats to travel between different bodies of water. They can be as simple as a ditch between two lakes, or as complex as a channel between two oceans.

» **Name:** Beijing-Hangzhou Grand Canal, Chi

## ailways

ains are a very useful
y of transporting people
d goods across land.
n average, a train carriage
es one-quarter of the fuel
rry uses. Railways also
lp lower road traffic.

» **Name:** Trans-Siberian Railway, Russia

## Buildings

Buildings protect people
and their possessions
from the cold, wind, and
rain. Civil engineers are in
charge of the structure of
a building, which allows it
to support weight and
stand up against weather.

**Name:** Tate Modern, London, UK

## ridges

gineers design bridges to
pport the weight of cars,
cks, trains, and people as
ey cross rivers, bays, and
nyons. Civil engineers
cide what type of bridge
best for the kind of traffic
will carry.

» **Name:** Danyang-Kunshan Great Bridge, China

## Dams

Dams block the flow of a
river, letting water build
up behind them to form a
lake. The flow of water
through the dam can then
be used to make electricity.

**Name:** Three Gorges Dam, China

# Underground

Engineers design important underground systems that keep cities running. Cables bring electricity to homes and businesses and pipes bring water and take away waste. Public transport moves thousands of people around much more quickly than cars can. Tunnels are buried where there are no buildings or traffic to get in the way. Take a look at what goes on under our feet!

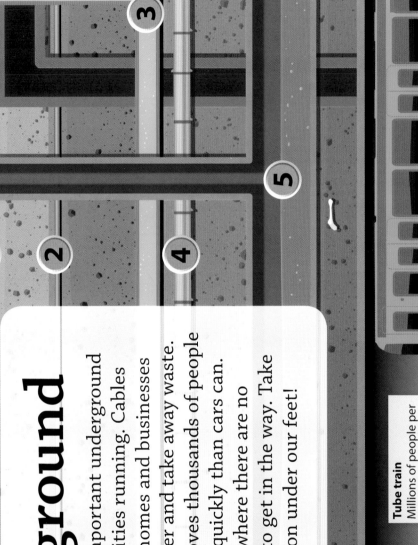

**1**

**2**

**3**

**4**

**5**

25 cm (10 in)

35 cm (15 in)

1 m (3.3 ft)

2 m (6.5 ft)

25 m (80 ft)

**6**

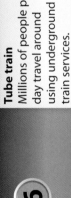

**Tube train**
Millions of people per day travel around using underground train services.

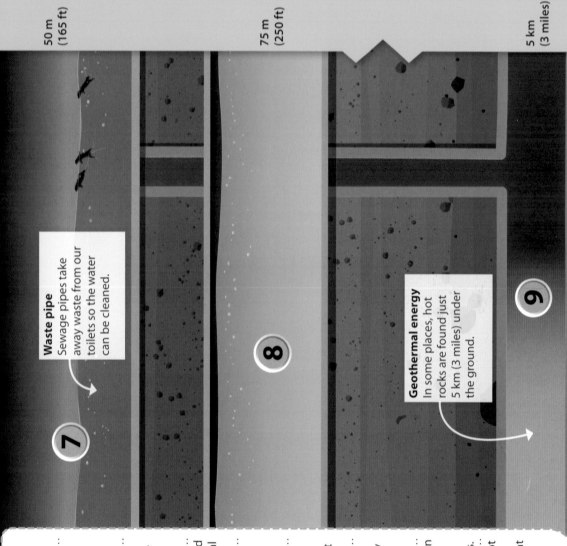

50 m
(165 ft)

75 m
(250 ft)

5 km
(3 miles)

**Waste pipe**
Sewage pipes take away waste from our toilets so the water can be cleaned.

**Geothermal energy**
In some places, hot rocks are found just 5 km (3 miles) under the ground.

(7)

(8)

(9)

>> **1. Telephone and electricity cables:** Electricity travels through miles of buried cable from power stations to houses, shops, and offices.

>> **2. Fibre-optic cable:** These cables use light to move information and energy around the city. Services like the Internet and television are connected using fibre-optic cables.

>> **3. Water mains:** Water mains are pipes that bring clean water to buildings such as houses. The water in the pipe is put under pressure to keep it moving fast around the network.

>> **4. Gas pipes:** Natural gas is used for cooking and heating. It is transported underground using metal pipes specially engineered for safety.

>> **5. Water drain:** Drainage systems are designed by engineers to prevent flooding as well as to circulate water from our toilets and sinks.

>> **6. Underground transport:** It is much faster to take a tube train than to drive! Underground train systems use deep tunnels under cities to transport millions of people without getting stuck in traffic.

>> **7. Sewer system:** Do you ever wonder where your waste goes when you flush the toilet? Gravity makes the water flow downwards to a treatment facility where it can be cleaned and re-used.

>> **8. Deep water mains:** A city's water supply often comes from underground rocks filled with water, called an aquifer. This is connected to the deep water mains then sent to smaller, local water pipes.

>> **9. Geothermal heating:** In some places with hot rocks near the surface, such as Iceland, engineers can pump water down into the Earth's crust to heat up. The water turns into steam, which is then used in power stations to create electricity.

# Eiffel Tower

Standing over Paris, the Eiffel Tower is one of the world's greatest engineering achievements. Built in 1889, it was the tallest structure in the world for four decades. More than 250 million people have visited the tower.

## Viewing platform

A staggering 276 m (906 ft) above the ground is a viewing platform. From here, visitors can enjoy breathtaking views of Paris and its other landmarks, such as the Arc de Triomphe.

## Lifts

The top level is accessed by two lifts. The distance covered by the lifts going up and down every year is the same as travelling around the world twice!

## Ironwork

This wrought-iron structure in a lattice design weighs about 10,000 tonnes (11,000 tons). Every seven years the ironwork is coated in 50 tonnes (55 tons) of paint to prevent rust.

The Eiffel Tower grows 15 cm (6 in) taller in hot weather!

- **Name:** Eiffel Tower
- **Country:** France
- **Height:** 321 m (1,052 ft)
- **Weight:** 10,000 tonnes (11,000 tons)

At the halfway stage

**Building up**
More than 300 builders worked for over two years on the project. A major part was to make the rivets that hold the pieces together.

Working on-site

**Tower of strength**
Guards, screens, and moving creeper cranes helped to support the structure and keep it safe for workers.

## Construction

The Eiffel Tower was designed to be a temporary entrance for the World's Fair in 1889, but it soon became permanent. Deep concrete and limestone foundations were laid first before the structure got under way.

Gustave Eiffel

**Creator**
The tower is named after engineer Gustave Eiffel whose company ran the project. Eiffel also helped design the Statue of Liberty in New York, USA.

45

# Skyscrapers

A skyscraper is a very tall building with lots of floors. Skyscrapers are so big that they have become landmarks all over the world.

These magnificent engineering structures take a long time to build, and a lot of careful planning to make sure everything is safe.

## Cranes

Skyscrapers would not be able to be built without cranes. These clever machines are very tall and are used to lift and transport materials.

## Lift shaft

In most skyscrapers, the lift shaft is built first. The lift is the building's central core and helps to keep it stable and safe.

The completed

## Beautiful building

Many skyscrapers are designed with curves, twists, and patterns to make them stand out from the rest. The Shard, in London, was designed to look like lots of shards of glass poking into the sky.

## Super structure

Skyscrapers are built in a giant 3D grid. This is called a super structure. It is like the building's skeleton.

of steel. Steel is strong and light, which makes it perfect for tall buildings. If the metal was too heavy, the building wouldn't be able to support itself.

## Curtain wall

The curtain wall covers the outside of the building. It is connected to the steel grid inside.

# Foundations

A foundation keeps the building stable, and protects it against wind and earthquakes. Skyscrapers have foundations made from concrete that go deep into the ground.

Under the Shard

**A long way down**
The Shard sits on top of many huge layers of concrete. These layers support the skyscraper's weight, and go down 53 m (174 ft).

# Building bridges

A bridge is a structure that lets people cross water, canyons, roads, or railways. Bridges often support heavy weights. They can be very long, and have to face challenges including wind, rain, and heavy traffic. When engineers design a bridge, they must make sure all the pieces fit together and balance properly.

## BASCULE

A bascule bridge has a section that can be raised or lowered to allow ships to pass through it. Bascule bridges have been used since ancient times – for example, as castle drawbridges.

## Arch

Arch bridges were first engineered by the Ancient Romans. The arch of the bridge run between two towers. The towers are where most of the weight is supported. Many arch bridges are used to carry railway lines.

## TRUSS

A truss bridge is created by fitting pieces of steel or wood together into triangle shapes called trusses. These carry the weight of the bridge. Trusses are very strong because each point of each triangle supports weight.

## Beam

A beam bridge is the simplest kind of bridge. It is a strong, metal plank with legs that go deep into the water or ground. A beam bridge is stiff, and does not bend or twist when a heavy vehicle crosses it.

# able-stayed

ble-stayed bridge has one or more towers.
n this tower, lots of support cables stretch
e bridge below. The cables fan out from
top of the tower to balance the weight of
ridge.

# Suspension

The road part of a suspension bridge hangs
from two tall towers. The tall towers are
secured deep under the water or ground
below, which keeps them strong. Long steel
cables connect the towers and the bridge.

**! WOW!**

The **Golden Gate Bridge** in San Francisco, USA, weighs **804,673 tonnes (887,000 tons)**.

# antilever

ntilever is a structure that is only supported at
end. A cantilever bridge is lots of these structures put
ther to make a crossing. They
easier to build than other
ges, as they don't need to be
ported when they are being
together.

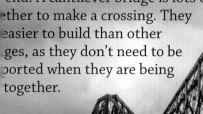

# Meet the expert

We put some questions to Dr Lucy Rogers, a Chartered Engineer, writer, and maker from the UK. Dr Rogers writes, experiments, makes engineering videos, and appears on engineering television shows.

**Q: We know it is something to do with engineering, but what is your actual job?**

**A:** I solve problems. Sometimes I calculate the probability of spacecraft being hit by space debris. Sometimes I make robot dinosaurs at a theme park react to visitors. I write articles for the European Space Agency, national newspapers and magazines. I work with engineering companies and make how-to videos. I am also a judge on BBC Robot Wars.

**Q: What made you decide to become an engineer?**

**A:** At school I really enjoyed making things. We had a "Great Egg Race" club, where we would have to solve problems. As I also like maths and physics, engineering was ideal.

**Q: Do you have a favourite thing that you have built?**

**A:** My latest project is often my favourite – currently my light-up gold boots. Anyone can change the colour of the lights by tweeting "#Cheerlights" and their favourite colour of the rainbow.

Dr Rogers enjoys working on experiments

Dr Rogers' latest project – light-up gold boo

## Do you use any special equipment?

My hands and imagination are the tools I value most. To make things, I use tools such as a lathe for shaping wood or metal, a solder for sticking metal together, and a 3D printer for making small plastic items. I also use a computer. This helps me draw things, calculate things, write stuff and also ask the internet for help. The Maker Community (people all around the world who make things) are also always willing to help and share ideas.

## What do you love most about engineering?

The buzz I get when I solve a problem for someone or something. Although most of my projects are fun, they demonstrate useful ideas. These ideas can be used in industry or the home. For example, my gold boots could be 100 machines in a factory that need to be controlled or checked all at once. This could be done not just from the factory, but even from another country.

## What is a usual work day for you?

I don't have a "usual" day – especially if I am on site, visiting factories, filming, or at a conference. Other times, I work from home. I don't have to be in an office. I like to get up early and do some writing before breakfast. This could be preparing a speech, writing a report or writing part of a book. After lunch I usually go into my workshop and make things. I spend a lot of the day

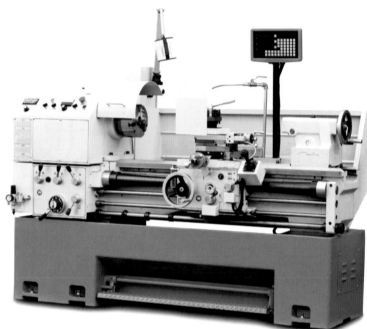

**Lathe**
Shapes metal and wood by spinning the material fast, and using a cutting tool over the surface in a regular pattern.

keeping my eye on Twitter and my emails too – this is how I talk to potential, current and past colleagues and clients.

**Q: What are the best and worst things about your job?**

**A:** The best thing is learning new stuff every day. I use my skills to make things and solve problems. The worst thing is being a beginner at new stuff every day – I want to skip the "learning" bit and immediately become an expert. Sadly, I have found no short cuts.

# Bioengineering

Bioengineers work on changes to the natural world. They research how our bodies work to create new medicines, and design inventions called prosthetics to replace missing body parts. Some bioengineers investigate farming and food technology.

### Lab-grown meat

In 2013, the world's first lab-grown burger was created. Engineers are working on ways to make it in larger batches and more cheaply – the burger cost £267,500 ($330,000) to create! The meat has the right texture but doesn't taste very good yet.

This meat was made from stem cells from a cow's shoulder.

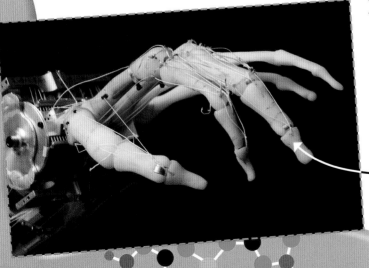

### Mechanical hand

Biomechanics is the science of how our bodies perform. Engineers can create mechanical body parts that are able to move and hold objects. They have also built running blades for athletes with missing feet or legs.

Mechanical parts can replace hands lost in accidents.

## rtificial heart

oengineers are working
create an entire artificial
art that can beat like a
al one. This is a huge
allenge – the human
art beats around 35
llion times a year so a
placement heart must be
ry strong and reliable.

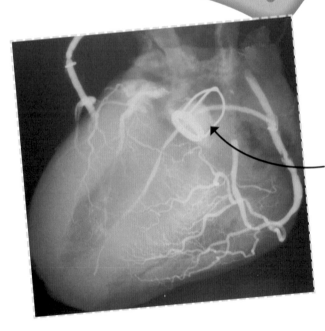

Some parts of the
heart can already
be replaced by
surgeons.

This calf was born
to cloned parents.

### Cloned cows

Researchers from
Texas, USA, have cloned
cows that make more,
better-quality meat than
average cows. Clones are
identical copies of animals.

## Food technology

Genetic engineers are creating animals
and plants that are more nutritious to eat
and can fight back against disease and
pests. Helping farmers grow more food
on the same amount of land could help
end hunger around the world.

# Going green

Engineers come up with ideas that will help the planet and our natural environment. They find new and creative ways to get rid of waste and save energy. Engineers also work on making new products that do not damage the world around us.

**Landfill repair**

This site was once where all of the rubbish from New York was dumped. It has now been cleaned up and specially engineered into a big park for local people. Trees have been planted and lakes created to make the area more attractive, healthier, and safer.

Fresh Kills landfill site, Staten Island, New York, USA

**Water straws**

A company in Switzerland has made a drinking straw that makes dirty water clean enough to drink. The straw has tiny fibres inside, which trap dirt, letting only clean water through. The straw is used by people who live in or explore areas without clean water.

The LifeStraw lets you drink dirty water safely.

LifeStraw

### Planting trees

In China, engineers have created a natural barrier against damaging dust storms. This "Great Wall" of trees is being planted on land that was once used to grow crops.

w forest in China

Wind farm in Australia

### Powerful wind turbines

Each wind turbine can power around 750 homes. Wind power is a form of renewable energy, or energy that can be used again, which doesn't harm the environment.

### Solar ovens

The heat of the Sun is so powerful it can be used to cook food. Silver-coloured reflectors can be used to focus the Sun's rays on a particular spot. It takes a long time to cook anything using this method, but it's better for the environment than using gas or electricity.

Food cooking in a solar oven

## Robot suits

These suits help injured people to walk again. The suit has several "walk modes" so patients can gradually recover from their injuries.

**Insect protein bars**

## Bug snacks

Insects are high in protein and easy to farm as they don't take up much space. Bugs are a food of the future!

Edible ins

*Robot suit*

# Future engineering

Engineers are always looking for new ways to create things that will help people. These are some new and exciting ideas that may soon become everyday sights.

## Self-driving cars

These cars are designed to drive themselves. They have computer sensors that monitor all sides so that they can drive safely without being controlled by anyone.

*There are no driving controls inside the ca*

## Solar roadways

This road surface works like a solar panel. It collects energy from the Sun that can be turned into electricity without harming the environment.

Solar roadway

## 3D printing

This process takes a computer design and turns it into a 3D object. The object is made by printing lots of layers on top of each other, using materials like plastic.

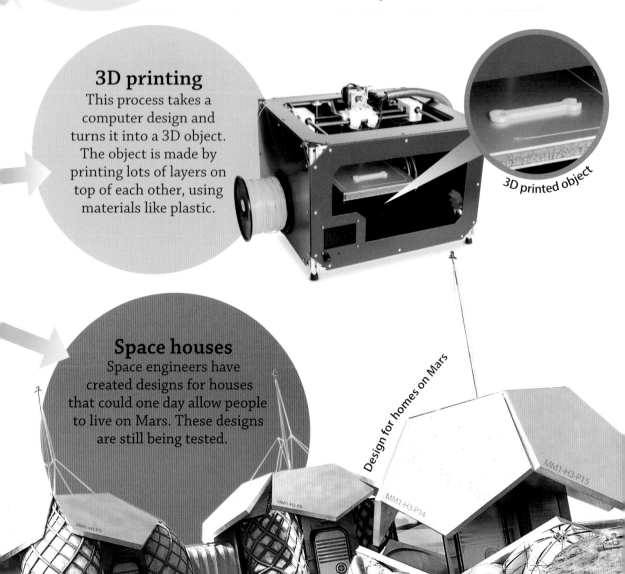

3D printed object

## Space houses

Space engineers have created designs for houses that could one day allow people to live on Mars. These designs are still being tested.

Design for homes on Mars

MM1-H1-P3

MM1-H2-P8

MM1-H3-P14

MM1-H3-P15

# Engineering facts and figures

The world of engineering is full of amazing things. Here are some weird and wonderful facts and figures that you may not know.

**The Pan-American Highway** is the longest road in the world. It is **48,000 km (30,000 miles)** long and connects North and South America.

**LONGEST ROAD!**

# HUNDREDS OF PEOPLE
**pushed blocks of stone uphill to** build the city of **Machu Picchu** in Peru, South America, around the year 1450.

# 25,572
strands of wire make up the cables of San Francisco's Golden Gate Bridge.

# 350
kph (220 mp[h] is the top spe[ed] of trains in China.

The world's **highest outdoor lift** is **Bailong** in China. It is **326 m (1,070 ft) tall.**

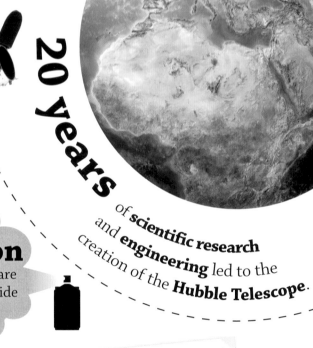

**20 years** of **scientific research** and **engineering** led to the creation of the **Hubble Telescope**.

**15 billion** **cans** of **aerosol** are produced worldwide **every year**.

Dubai's Palm Islands are the **biggest man-made islands** in the world.

# 1863

s the year the first derground railway ened, in London. was called the etropolitan Railway.

# 3.9°

is the angle of the Leaning Tower of Pisa. Its foundations were laid in soft soil that could not support its weight, so it tipped to one side.

# Glossary

Here are the meanings of some words that are useful for you to know when learning all about engineering, from bridges to spaceships.

**accelerate** To speed up

**aerospace engineering** Projects to do with aircraft and spacecraft

**android** Robot with a human face

**astronaut** Someone who is trained to travel and work in a spacecraft

**atom** Smallest part of something that can take part in a chemical reaction

**automatic** Something that works on its own without human help

**bioengineering** Technology that is used to help the human body

**cantilever** Bridge that is only supported at one end

**chemical** Substance made by a reaction between particles such as atoms

**chemical engineering** Science that uses chemicals to make new products

**civil engineering** Designing projects such as bridges and roads

**combustion** Process of burning

**composites** Something made from several parts or materials

**coolant** Liquid or gas that cools things down

**debris** Bits of broken-up a loose material

**design** To plan and work o how something will work and what it will look like

**drone** Flying machine with no pilot

**eco** To do with not harmin the natural environment

**energy** Source of power such as electrical energy or heat energy

**environment** Area that someone lives in, or that a machine works in

**environmental engineerir** Projects to do with the wo around us

**fibre-optic** Cables that are used to move light signals

**fossil fuels** Fuels made fro animals and plants that die millions of years ago, for example coal

**geothermal** Heat that comes from inside the Eart

**humanoid** Robot that loo and moves like a human

**hydraulic power** When something is moved by wa or another liquid

Civil engineering includes roads

**...ernational Space ...tion (ISS)** Large space ...tion and laboratory ...t orbits the Earth

**...chine** Something that ...owered by energy and ...sed to carry out a task

**...nufactured** Made by ...mans rather than ...wn naturally

**...terial** Substance that ...sed to make or build ...ngs

**...chanical** Something ...t is controlled by a ...chine

**...chanical engineering** ...gineering that makes ...d designs machines

**...notechnology** Science ...t deals with making ...hnology very small

**...clear-powered** Action ...t is powered by nuclear ...rgy

**...rticle** Something that ...ery small, such as a ...oton or electron

**...wer source** Energy that ...sed to make a machine ...rk, such as electricity

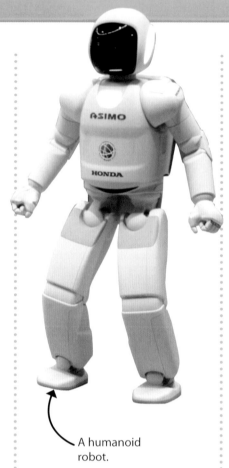

A humanoid robot.

**prosthetic** Artificial body part to replace one that is missing

**renewable** Type of energy that can be produced without polluting the air or water, such as solar power

**robot** Machine that is programmed by a computer to do different tasks

**satellite** Any object that goes around the Earth, but often a manufactured machine that collects scientific information

**software** Programs and instructions that are used by a computer

**structure** Building that is made up of several parts

**sustainable** Energy or materials that can keep going for a long time

**synthetic** Something that is man-made

**technology** Using scientific knowledge to create machinery and devices, such as computers

**thrust** Forward motion

**transfer** When energy is moved from one object to another, or an object moves from one place to another

**transform** When something turns into something else, for example changing shape

**turbine** Wheel or rotor that is turned to make power

**wind tunnel** Tunnel that lets engineers see the effect of wind on objects such as cars or bikes

# Index

3D printing  57

**A**

aerosols  59
Agrawal, Roma  23
aircraft  4, 25, 28–29, 30–31,
      32–33
aircraft carriers  25
androids  20
animals  53
aqueducts  11
aquifers  43
arch bridges  48
astronauts  37

**B**

bacteria  34
bandages  34
bascule bridges  48
batteries  17
beam bridges  48
Bell, Alexander Graham  23
bioengineering  52–53
biomechanics  52
body parts, prosthetic  21,
      22, 52
bridges  41, 48–49, 58
Brunel, Isambard Kingdom  22
buildings  11, 23, 41, 46–47,
      55, 58

**C**

cables  5, 42, 43
cable-stayed bridges  49
canals  40
cantilever bridges  49
carbon  35
cars  16–17, 56

ceramics  12
chemicals  38–39
civil engineers  40
clones  53
clothes  12, 39
coal  18–19, 39
composite materials  13, 28
computers  51
concrete  13
cows, cloned  53
cranes  14, 25, 46

**D**

dams  18, 19, 41
diggers  14–15
drains  43
drills  24
drinking water  10, 54
driverless vehicles  15, 56
drones  29
Dubai  14, 59

**E**

Eiffel, Gustave  45
Eiffel Tower, Paris  44–45
electric cars  17
electricity  10, 13, 18–19, 41,
      43, 57
electricity cables  42, 43
engineers  8–9, 22–23
engines, jet  32–33
environment  38, 54–55
extreme machines  24–25

**F**

fabrics  12, 35
factories  20
farming  15, 52, 53

feelings  21
fibre-optic cables  43
flying machines  28–29, 30–3
      32–33
food technology  38, 52, 53,
fossil fuels  18–19
foundations, buildings  47
future engineering  56–57

**G**

gantry cranes  25
gas  18, 39
gas pipes  43
genetic engineers  53
geothermal power  18–19, 43
Gilbreth, Lillian Moller  22
gliders  31
Golden Gate Bridge, San
      Francisco  49, 58
graphene  35

**H**

Hadron Collider  25
hands, prosthetic  21, 22, 52
heart, artificial  53
helicopters  29
houses, on Mars  57
Hubble Telescope  59
Hudson Yards, New York  11
humanoid robots  20
hydraulic power  14
hydroelectricity  19, 41

**I**

insects  56
International Space Station
      (ISS)  36
Internet  43

nwork 44
nds, artificial 59

aircraft 28, 32–33
acks 14
bo jets 32–33

hens 22

dfill sites 54
nes 51
ning Tower of Pisa 59
nardo da Vinci 8–9
ers 7
s 44, 46, 59

chines 14–15
chu Picchu, Peru 58
rs 4, 37, 57
terials 12–13, 35, 36, 39
tsuoka, Yoky 22
at 52, 53
dicine 34, 38, 52–53
tals 13

otechnology 34–35
SA 25
lear power 18–19
lear submarines 24

18

n Islands, Dubai 59
-American Highway 40, 58
achutes 9

particle accelerators 25
pipes 42–43
plants 53, 55
plastics 12, 39, 57
power stations 18–19
problem solving 4, 10–11,
   50–51
prosthetics 21, 22, 52
public transport 42
pylons, electricity 18

**R**
railways 23, 41, 43, 48, 58
refrigerators 10
renewable energy 55
roads 24, 40, 57, 58
road trains 24
robotic arms 15, 36
robots 20–21, 50
robot suits 56
rockets 37
Rogers, Dr Lucy 50–51
roller coasters 26–27
rovers, space 37

**S**
satellites 10
self-driving vehicles 15, 56
sewers 21, 43
The Shard, London 23, 46–47
ships 22, 25
silicone 35
skyscrapers 11, 46–47
solar power 18–19, 36, 39, 57
Soyuz space craft 11
spacecraft 11, 37, 50
space engineers 23, 36–37
space houses 57
spacesuits 37
speed 16, 17, 58
steam power 18, 43
steel 47

Stephenson, George 23
submarines 24
sun protection 34
suspension bridges 49
synthetic chemicals 38

**T**
telephones 10, 23, 43
telescopes 5, 59
television 10, 43
tiltrotor aircraft 29
towers 44–45, 48, 49, 59
tractors, driverless 15
trains 23, 41, 43, 48, 58
transport 40–41, 42, 43, 56
trucks 24
truss bridges 48
tube trains 42, 43, 59
tunnels 24, 40, 42
turbines 10, 18–19, 55, 58
turbofans 33
tyres 16, 17

**U**
underground railways 42, 43,
   59
underground systems 42–43

**W**
Walkie Talkie building 11
waste pipes 43
water 10, 11
water mains 43
water power 14, 18–19, 41
waterproof fabrics 35, 39
water straws 54
wave power 18
weapons 9
wind power 10, 18–19, 39, 55,
   58
wood 13
Wright brothers 28, 30–31

# Acknowledgements

The author would like to thank her friend and fellow engineer, Benton Allen, for all of his great ideas and help. The publisher would like to thank the following people for their assistance in the preparation of this book: Dan Crisp for illustrations; Bettina Myklebust Stovne for design assistance; Caroline Hunt for proofreading; Hilary Bird for compiling the index; and Dr Lucy Rogers for her "Meet the expert" interview.

The publisher would like to thank the following for their kind permission to reproduce their photographs:

(Key: a-above; b-below/bottom; c-centre; f-far; l-left; r-right; t-top)

1 Getty Images: Mark Runnacles (c). 2 123RF.com: 8vfanrf (bl). 3 Alamy Stock Photo: Victor Wallner (cb). Dorling Kindersley: Claire Cordier and Claire Cordier and Claire Cordier (r/Shard). 4 Alamy Stock Photo: imageBROKER (cr). Getty Images: Luis Alvarez (cl). 5 Alamy Stock Photo: Jake Lyell (cl). Dreamstime.com: Monkey Business Images (br). NASA: (tr). 6 Alamy Stock Photo: Classic Image (br). 7 123RF.com: Patrick Guenette (br). Dreamstime.com: Ken Backer (ca). 8 Alamy Stock Photo: Photo Researchers, Inc (l). 9 Alamy Stock Photo: Photo12 (ca). Getty Images: Fabrice Coffrini / AFP (tr); Science & Society Picture Library (b). 10 123RF.com: Dimitar Marinov / oorka (cl). Alamy Stock Photo: Richard Levine (cr). NASA: JPL-Caltech (ca). 11 iStockphoto.com: IR_Stone (ca). NASA: (cla). 12-13 Alamy Stock Photo: wendy connett. 12 Dreamstime.com: Edite Artmann (b); Okea (c). 13 Dreamstime.com: Pakkano (crb). 14 Dorling Kindersley: Richard Leeney / Patrick Racing, CART, 2001 (cla). Dreamstime.com: Dmitry Kalinovsky (tr). 15 CNH Industrial: (crb). Dreamstime.com: Kittipong Jirasukhanont (c); Wellphotos (cra). 17 Dreamstime.com: Danil Roudenko (tl). 18 Corbis: Westend61 / Fotofeeling (bl). 19 Alamy Stock Photo: Greg Vaughn (ca); Helene ROCHE Photography (c); Robertharding (cb); Reuters / Ruben Sprich (b). 20 123RF.com: Vladimir Salman (crb). Alamy Stock Photo: Chris Willson (cla). Dreamstime.com: Neil Denize (clb). 21 Getty Images: Mark Runnacles (cla, c). Science Photo Library: Peter Menzel (cra, crb, cb). 22 Alamy Stock Photo: Bygone Collection (cl); Tatu (tr); Rachel Husband (cra). Getty Images: Underwood Archives (clb). University of Washington: (crb, br). 23 Alamy Stock Photo: Chronicle (tl); WENN Ltd (clb). Dreamstime.com: Claudiodivizia (cla); Georgios Kollidas (tr). Getty Images: Underwood Archives (cra). Science Photo Library: David Nunuk (bl). 24 Alamy Stock Photo: qaphotos.com (cra). Dorling Kindersley: Graham Rae / Royal Naval Submarine Museum (b). iStockphoto.com: John Kirk (cr). 25 Alamy Stock Photo: Leslie Wilk (cr); Stocktrek Images, Inc. (b). NASA: Tony Landis (cla). 26-27 Cedar Point. 26 Cedar Point: (ca). Getty Images: Mathew Imaging /

WireImage (br). 27 Getty Images: Topical Press Agency (bc). 28 Alamy Stock Photo: Bailey-Cooper Photography (cb); Susan & Allan Parker (cr). Dorling Kindersley: Royal Airforce Museum, London (cla). 29 Alamy Stock Photo: Ian Dagnall (cra); Johnny Henshall (cr); Victor Wallner (cb). 32-33 Alamy Stock Photo: Andrew Holt. 32 Getty Images: Pascal Pavani / AFP (bc). 34 Science Photo Library: Steve Gschmeissner (l, r). 35 Dreamstime.com: Kts (cl). Science Photo Library: Andre Geim, Kostya Novoselov (l); Eye of Science (r). 36-37 Science Photo Library: NASA. 37 Dorling Kindersley: NASA (ca). NASA: JPL / Cornell University (crb). 38 Dreamstime.com: Huguette Roe (bl). 39 Alamy Stock Photo: Cultura Creative (RF) (bl). Dreamstime.com: Broker (br); Monkey Business Images (bc). 40 Alamy Stock Photo: Hemis (clb); Reuters / Arnd Wiegmann (cra); Meng Delong / Xinhua (br). 41 Alamy Stock Photo: artsimages (cla); Horizons WWP / TRVL (tr); John Henshall (bl). Getty Images: LUPOO / ullstein bild (crb). 44 Alamy Stock Photo: AGF Srl (ca). 44-45 Alamy Stock Photo: allOver images. 45 Alamy Stock Photo: Chronicle (cra); Pictorial Press Ltd (tr). Getty Images: Bettmann (cr). 46-47 Alamy Stock Photo: Ian Macpherson London. 46 Alamy Stock Photo: Ian Macpherson London (crb). Dorling Kindersley: (tr). 47 Alamy Stock Photo: Gale S. Hanratty (cr). 48 Dreamstime.com: Arsty (bl); Len Green (crb). 49 Dreamstime.com: Hel080808 (cl); Ilya Genkin (tl). Getty Images: Loop Images / UIG (b). 50 Dr Lucy Rodgers: (All images). 51 Dreamstime.com: Andrey Eremin (cra). 52 Getty Images: John Kuczala (bl). 53 University of Washington: (bl). 53 Science Photo Library: (ca). Whitley Sprague/ West Texas A&M University: (clb). 54-55 123RF.com: Shannon Fagan (t). 54 Alamy Stock Photo: Richard Levine (c). Dorling Kindersley: Vestergaard Frandsen (cb). 55 Dreamstime.com: David Steele (cra). Getty Images: Fadel Senna / AFP (crb). 56 Alamy Stock Photo: epa european pressphoto agency b.v. (cl); Ton Koene (tc, cra). BMW Group: (crb, br). 57 123RF.com: 8vfanrf (cr). Foster + Partners: (b). Solar Roadways: (t). 58 Dreamstime.com: Jarnogz (cra). 59 123RF.com: Konstantin Stepanenko (cr). Dorling Kindersley: Andy Crawford (tc). Dreamstime.com: Greatandaman (l). 60 Alamy Stock Photo: Hemis (bl). Getty Images: Loop Images / UIG (tl). 61 Dreamstime.com: Neil Denize (tc). 62 Dorling Kindersley: (tl)

Endpapers: Front: Alamy Stock Photo: National Geographic Creative br; Corbis: Westend61 /

Fotofeeling c; Dreamstime.com: Anton Samso iMac® is a trademark of Apple Inc., registered in U.S. and other countries bc, Nataliya Hora cr; N JPL bl; Back: akg-images: Hervé Champollion tl; Alamy Stock Photo: Granger Historical Picture Archive cla; Dorling Kindersley: R. Florio bc, Th Science Museum, London tc, cb; Getty Images cra; NASA: JPL-Caltech crb; Wikipedia: Gabriel Vanin clb

Cover images: Front: 123RF.com: Dimitar Mar oorka fcr; Alamy Stock Photo: Ian Dagnall fcra, N Saracco crb; Dorling Kindersley: The National Railway Museum, York / Science Museum Grou Dreamstime.com: Andrey Eremin c, Kittipong Jirasukhanont bc; iStockphoto.com: Naumoid t NASA: cla, JPL-Caltech cra; Back: Alamy Stock Photo: Susan &amp Allan Parker tr, Victor Walln Dorling Kindersley: Peter Rowe and Dave Pea of Kawazaki Robotics Ltd cl; Front Flap: 123RF. 8vfanrf clb; Alamy Stock Photo: Andrew Holt c european pressphoto agency b.v. c; Dorling Kindersley: bc, Andy Crawford cl, Vestergaard Frandsen ca/ (Lifestraw); Getty Images: Mark Runnacles cr; University of Washington: bl; B Flap: Getty Images: Nash Photos clb; NASA: cr

All other images © Dorling Kindersley
For further information see: www.dkimages

My Findout facts:

# Types of engineering

## Civil

**Key features**

Civil engineers build roads, bridges, tunnels, and buildings.

Most civil engineers work with construction and transport workers.

Suspension bridge

## Mechanical

**Key features**

Mechanical engineers design and build machines.

Roller coasters, space telescopes, and robots are all made by mechanical engineers.

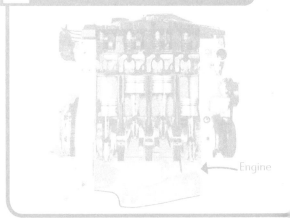

Engine

## Aerospace

**Key features**

Aerospace engineers design and build machines that fly.

Planes, helicopters, rockets, and spacecraft are all created by aerospace engineers.

Mars Curiosity rover

## Software

**Key features**

Software engineers design computer software and devices.

Computer games, video calling, and robots are all coded by software engineers.

Website